'No more than an octagonal shelter,

but a perfect piece of garden architecture,

both precise and playful. A cedar-shingled,

bell-shaped roof commands the axis

yet charms the eye in every chance view

glimpsed through the trees.'

FRANK WALKER, 2005

LOCH FYNE

N

Strachur
River Cur

GLENBRANTER

LOCH GOIL

Glen Shellish

Whistlefield

GLENFINART

Bernice

Beinn Mhor
(Benmore)
2437

Coirantee

Clach Beinn
2109

Glenfinart Ho.

Glen Masson

Ardentinny

Inverchapel
1798
Stronchullin
Hill

River Echaig

BENMORE HOUSE
& POLICIES
ARBORETUM

Gairletter

BENMORE

LOCH LONG

PUCKSGLEN

FORESTGARDEN

Blairmore

Kilmun

HOLY LOCH

Strone Pt.

Sandbank

Pier
Hunter's Quay

LOCH STRIVE

KIRN
Pier

Scale of Miles

1   0   1   2   3

DUNOON
Pier

DAVID GRAY

CHERISHED PLAN

The Story of Puck's Hut at Benmore

Royal Botanic Garden Edinburgh

2020

First published in 2020 by the
Royal Botanic Garden Edinburgh
with generous support from the
Younger (Benmore) Trust

Celebrating
350
1670 · 2020

Royal
Botanic Garden
Edinburgh

ISBN 978-1-910877-35-7

The Royal Botanic Garden Edinburgh (RBGE) is a
registered Scottish charity (SC007983) and a Non
Departmental Public Body (NDPB) sponsored
and supported through Grant-in-Aid by the
Scottish Government's Environment and Forestry
Directorate (ENFOR). RBGE also has a legal status
as an academic institution.

The Younger (Benmore) Trust is a charity
registered in Scotland (number SC000284)

This is a carbon-balanced publication. The carbon
impact of this document has been offset with a carbon
capture charge at a rate of £8.50 per tonne of paper
(equivalent to approximately 2p per ream of A4 80gsm
or 12p per ream of SRA2 100gsm). Premier Paper
Group will pay all Carbon Capture charges directly to
the Woodland Trust, a charity registered in England,
Wales and Scotland. Supporting the Woodland Trust
helps capture CO_2 and plant trees.

Designed and typeset in Kingfisher
by Nye Hughes, Dalrymple
Printed by Gomer Press Ltd, Wales

Front cover: Detail of postcard of Puck's Hut, Puck's
Glen, near Dunoon c.1935. Private collection [fig.22]

Frontispiece: Map showing locations of Puck's Glen,
Benmore and Glenbranter. Reproduced from *Benmore:
A Guide to the Younger Botanic Garden at Benmore,
Argyllshire*. John Macqueen Cowan (1937).
Image reproduced courtesy of RBGE Library &
Archive Services.

Back cover: Detail of memorial carved ceiling rose,
2020. Photograph by Sybil Gray.

Contents

Foreword

The progress of the Royal Botanic Garden Edinburgh (RBGE) and its people is marked by many milestones, plant introductions, scientific discoveries and buildings. This is the story of one of our more extraordinary buildings: a memorial at Benmore known as Puck's Hut. It celebrates the life of Sir Isaac Bayley Balfour, 9th Regius Keeper of RBGE and an outstanding academic, inspiring teacher and visionary. He was knighted for his research into the moss genus *Sphagnum*, which was to help save the lives of many thousands of injured troops. It is thanks to Balfour that RBGE would re-emerge from the tragedy of global conflict as one of the great botanical gardens in the world.

Balfour saw the need for a satellite garden in the west of Scotland whose climate would allow trees and newly discovered species to thrive. He saw too that trees were a key factor in controlling climate change. He died in 1922 before a suitable site could be developed, and there is a first memorial to him at the Edinburgh Garden dating from 1925. Puck's Hut was built three years later in a place he would have loved.

SIMON MILNE MBE
Regius Keeper, Royal Botanic Garden Edinburgh

Introduction

In January 1925, Royal Botanic Garden Edinburgh (RBGE) Regius Keeper William Wright Smith (1875–1956) identified a site to accommodate a planned memorial dedicated to the life of his predecessor Sir Isaac Bayley Balfour (1853–1922). Wright Smith wrote to Lady Agnes Balfour (1857–1940): 'Sir Robert Lorimer came down to see me last Sunday and we inspected various sites in the garden [at Inverleith]. The one which found most favour was on the wall near the big Cedar of Lebanon'.

A ceremonial unveiling performed by Sir Herbert Maxwell (1845–1937) some 18 months later revealed 'a slab of grey freestone … built into the wall encircling the terrace below the plant houses'. The surviving tablet, which would later be relocated, bears the following heartfelt inscription:

> THIS STONE COMMEMORATES
> SIR ISAAC BAYLEY BALFOUR
> KEEPER OF THESE GARDENS
> 1888–1922
> AND IS SET HERE BY HIS COLLEAGUES
> AND FRIENDS TO RECORD THE ZEAL
> WITH WHICH HE WORKED AND THE
> AFFECTION WHICH THEY BORE HIM

The Gardeners' Chronicle ran an illustrated report which praised 'the simplicity and restraint' exhibited by the tablet and its early setting. However, by the time of the Edinburgh dedication service a further plan to celebrate the lifelong achievements of Sir Isaac Bayley Balfour was well underway. The proposed location would be the remote west coast of Scotland, where, free from protocol and formality, the rugged rain-soaked Argyllshire landscape inspired the considerable imagination of Sir Robert Lorimer to create a modest but much-loved architectural gem.

Lorimer designed the timber framed and clad Sir Isaac Bayley Balfour Memorial Rest House familiar to most visitors at Benmore as Puck's Hut [fig.1]. It may be a surprise to learn that the present site in the Walled Garden was not the original location for the structure. The full context of Lorimer's design emerges from an extended narrative which sets out in some detail the background story to the origins of RBGE at Benmore.

Many of the intricacies surrounding the construction of Puck's Hut have long since faded from living memory. It is fortunate that original documents and the extensive cast of characters involved survive within numerous public archives making it possible to review, for the first time, this relatively minor but significant commission that arrived late in the career of Sir Robert Lorimer.

The Sir Isaac Bayley Balfour Memorial Rest House recognises the public service and lifetime accomplishment of a remarkable and dynamic individual. However, as will be revealed, the structure is also a symbol of a much wider movement and determined effort to reforest Scotland, placing Puck's Hut at the heart of long-term national strategies promoting the value of tree planting and the development of gardens, arboreta, woodlands and forests – the significance of which is perhaps only now being truly realised.

Fig.1 | *Colour postcard view. Puck's Hut (Bayley Balfour Memorial) and lower slopes from Walled Garden, c.1990. Private collection.*

Sir Isaac Bayley Balfour

Sir Isaac Bayley Balfour and RBGE

By every measurable standard Sir Isaac Bayley Balfour [fig.2] is recalled and celebrated as 'a most eminent botanist of any age'. Fate and circumstance conspired to determine that, as the son of a serving Regius Keeper, John Hutton Balfour (1808–84), the young Isaac was raised in and around the environs of RBGE. Perhaps unsurprisingly, natural science proved to be a stimulus, and he graduated from the University of Edinburgh in 1873. Duties as botanist and geologist on the Royal Society's 1874 astronomical expedition to Rodriguez Island (now Rodrigues Island, part of Mauritius) to observe the transit of Venus presented a unique opportunity. The trip to the southern seas yielded primary source material that allowed Bayley Balfour to complete his studies and gain his DSc in botany the following year. During the winter of 1879–80 he was once again on his travels, spending seven weeks on the island of Socotra. Data and specimens gathered on this trip would become the basis for the later *Botany of Socotra* (1888).

In 1879 Bayley Balfour was appointed Regius Professor of Botany at the University of Glasgow. The position afforded him the opportunity to advance his personal skills and gain administrative experience; a notable task at this time involved establishing a Winter Garden within the enlarged Kibble Palace following the relocation of the structure to the West End of Glasgow. A four-year tenure as Sherardian Professor of Botany at the University of Oxford followed before Bayley Balfour returned to his native city of Edinburgh in 1888 to undertake the dual roles of University Professor of Botany and Crown Professor and Keeper of the Garden. Soon after his appointment he became embroiled in lengthy bureaucratic negotiations which ultimately led to major administrative restructuring. The outcome (as Bayley Balfour desired) placed the Inverleith site under Public Parks Regulations. The resultant opening of the garden on Sundays – which provoked an acrimonious response from the infuriated Free Church Presbytery – proved to be a great success with the general public. Throughout the forthcoming decades Bayley Balfour devoted his life to modernising every aspect of the garden. His legacy would be the creation of a scientific and educational institution of the first order.

Botanical discoveries from collections made by men such as Sir Joseph Hooker (1817–1911), Karl Maximowich (1827–91) and Père Jean-Marie Delavay (1834–95) had alerted Bayley Balfour to the possibility of horticultural treasures yet to be gathered from the Far East. Always questing for knowledge, he paid a visit to Japan and China in 1909–10 with the aim of gaining familiarity with eastern Asiatic cultural conditions. This personal interest in the diverse flora of western China, particularly the genera *Primula* and *Rhododendron*, would pay a rich dividend. His organisational skill and sound judgement in appointing key members of staff resulted in RBGE establishing a reputation as the leading authority on Sino-Himalayan plants.

Fig.2 | *Sir Isaac Bayley Balfour (1853–1922). University Professor of Botany and Crown Professor and Keeper of RBGE. Image reproduced courtesy of RBGE Library & Archive Services.*

The outbreak of war in 1914 brought challenges well beyond Bayley Balfour's expected range of duties. Working with Edinburgh surgeon Charles Cathcart (1853–1932), he had discovered in 1914 that dried *Sphagnum* (bog moss) makes highly absorptive antiseptic wound dressings. Throughout the duration of the war Bayley Balfour diverted garden resources to help identify suitable locations for moss collection. By 1918 over one million dressings were used by British hospitals each month. The conflict would, however, bring personal tragedy to Bayley Balfour with the loss of his only son at Gallipoli in June 1915.

Bayley Balfour was created KBE shortly before retiring in 1922 to Haslemere in Surrey where he hoped for improvement in his physical health and planned to pursue his interests at a more leisurely pace with the part-time study and description of specimens gathered from China. A few months later his untimely death prompted many obituaries which affirmed his exceptional character and leadership skills.

Forestry Campaigner

At the age of 23 Bayley Balfour became a member of the Royal Scottish Arboricultural Society. Elected to the role of Society President (1890–3) he utilised his position to campaign for State-organised model experimental forests. He applied further pressure by demanding to know why there were no scientific (forestry) men on the staff of the Board of Agriculture.

In 1894 he was appointed President of the British Association for the Advancement of Science (Biological Section). Predictably, he chose forestry as the subject of his major address at Oxford. Demonstrating an impressive range of knowledge, he highlighted the neglect of forestry as a science and, as a direct consequence, missed economic opportunities. He touched upon many topics, including the adverse effects of forest exhaustion and a need for 'proper conservancy of forest areas'. He saw an urgent need for increased tree planting, firstly to offset worldwide overharvesting and demand, thereafter to harness the benefit of 'hygienic and climatic influences upon atmospheric conditions'. His resonant tone and citing of elementary science delivered a prescient message of continuing relevance to the modern world:

… the direct influence of tree-growth upon climate is no mere superstition … like all green plants, trees exercise, through the process of carbon-assimilation, a purifying effect upon the air … forests reduce the extremes of temperature of the air; they protect and control the water flow from the soil.

Fig.3 | *Emblem for the Royal Scottish Arboricultural Society and motto 'Ye may be aye sticking in a tree. It will be growing when ye're sleeping.' Image reproduced courtesy of Royal Scottish Forestry Society.*

Bayley Balfour went on to identify a shortage of skilled operatives and to lament the lack of investment in forestry training. He closed by urging a practical application and mobilisation of the science of botany: 'to botanists we must look in the first instance for the propagation of the scientific knowledge upon which this large industry must rest'. He backed up his rhetoric by personally delivering a short course of lectures on botany and forestry for practical foresters in the winter of 1890–1. He extended this initiative by setting up a two-year course of instruction for practical foresters at RBGE. From 1892 onward successful candidates gained paid employment in the garden or in local nurseries, with lectures available for free in the evenings. Bayley Balfour persuaded the Board of Agriculture to agree to meet the annual £150 tutoring fees.

Forestry in Scotland

The extent and destruction of Scotland's natural woodland cover has been long debated. Forestry historian and writer Chris Smout (b.1933) quotes (with some well-placed caution) the very rough estimate made by Walker and Kirby (1989) 'that by the end of the middle ages only about 4 percent of the Scottish land surface was covered by wood'. From the early 1600s onward landowners became increasingly interested in tree planting as a secure (if not very lucrative) long-term investment. The availability and demand for manuals such as *A Treatise on Forest Trees* (1775) and *The Forester* (1847) encouraged many successful attempts at large-scale planting. However, despite the determined effort of many improving or enlightened landowners and their foresters, the pathway to national reforestation remained elusive and uncertain.

Described succinctly as 'a self-styled prestigious lobby for progressive forestry',

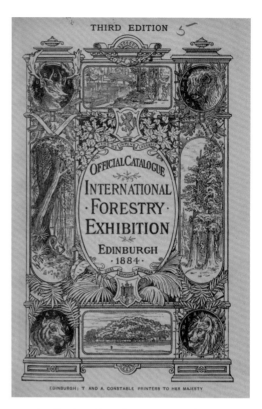

Fig.4 | *Official catalogue for International Forestry Exhibition Edinburgh 1884. Image reproduced courtesy of National Library of Scotland.*

the Royal Scottish Arboricultural Society [fig.3] was formed in 1854 and aimed 'to put [national] forestry on a proper footing'. In 1884 the organisation hosted the International Forestry Exhibition [fig.4] in the grounds of Donaldson's Hospital in Edinburgh. The event proved a public relations triumph, attracting in excess of half a million visitors over a three-month period. Momentum towards State forestry gained further impetus from major landowners such as the 16th Lord Lovat (Simon Fraser, 1871–1933) and Sir John Stirling Maxwell (1866–1956). Both men applied a scientific or systematic approach to forestry. Stirling Maxwell adapted pioneering methods at his Corrour estate in Inverness-shire to establish a forest upon elevated and peaty grounds. Lord Lovat was co-author of *The Great Glen Survey* (1911) which proposed the location as a suitable site for demonstration forest purposes. Their experience shaped the outlook and early policy of the fledgling Forestry Commission.

In the last days of the Liberal government led by Herbert Henry Asquith (1852–1928) a committee under the chairmanship of Francis Dyke Acland (1874–1939) recommended the introduction of State-organised forestry. M.L. Anderson (1895–1961) reflected in his *History of Scottish Forestry* (1967) that it had taken 'the global crisis of 1914–18 to finally emphasise that forestry in any country is a major land-use and an important element in the national economy'. The Forestry Commission was vested on 1 September 1919. The primary aim was the establishment of a strategic reserve of timber with exotic species introduced on an unprecedented scale.

In the aftermath of further global conflict (1939–45) an advisory enquiry of 1957 put forward the case for amenity and recreational considerations concluding that it was perhaps 'less meaningful to consider forestry policy in relation to war-time needs than in a primarily economic and social light'. This approach to reform was based partly upon the successful outcome of early trials pioneered on the uplands of Cowal and Argyll.

Botanical Introductions and George Forrest

While forestry in Scotland was being developed, the decades around the start of the 20th century also witnessed the introduction of an extraordinary wealth of trees and shrubs into Britain, predominantly from the temperate regions of East Asia. As might be expected, the national botanic garden of Scotland played an active role. Falkirk-born George Forrest (1873–1932) had accepted the post of Herbarium Assistant at RBGE in September 1903. The following year cotton merchant and nurseryman Arthur K. Bulley (1861–1942) of Neston, Cheshire, wrote to Bayley Balfour looking to secure the services of a suitable individual to undertake botanical exploration in western China. Forrest was recommended. He would eventually undertake seven expeditions, compiling an estimated 31,000 herbarium vouchers and introducing hundreds of new plants to cultivation. As a horticulturist, Bayley Balfour instinctively knew that such plants would not flourish within urban areas or on the east coast of Scotland. Throughout the last decade of his working life he sought a suitable location to allow successful cultivation of these plants. Failing health prompted him to reveal in a candid letter to a friend: 'but for the engineering of these schemes chiefly I should have bid my adieu at once on settlement after the war with the prospect of a good time in retirement'.

It was the outstanding success of Forrest as a plant collector that helped persuade Bayley Balfour of the need to establish a planting site, with abundant rainfall, in the west of Scotland. The acquisition of large tracts of land by the State under the Forestry Act (1919) offered a chance which Sir Isaac was quick to seize. A simultaneous plan to develop a high-altitude alpine garden within Caenlochan deer forest in the Cairngorms would remain unfulfilled.

The Search for a Suitable Site

Glenbranter

In October 1920 a chance gathering offered Sir Isaac Bayley Balfour the opportunity to put forward his case for what would become the first of RBGE's Regional Gardens. Present at the impromptu meeting was Chairman of the newly formed Forestry Commission the 16th Lord Lovat, Assistant Commissioner for Scotland John D. Sutherland (1865–1952) and host Sir John Stirling Maxwell. Exceptionally well connected and influential, all three men were veterans of the Acland committee. Taking advantage of the occasion, Bayley Balfour highlighted the role of RBGE and the study of *Rhododendrons* together with the need to identify a location where the more tender species could be grown, and

seen by students and the general public. The discussions were brief. The matter was settled in five minutes. It only remained to select a suitable site. In January 1923 Stirling Maxwell reported that 'an informal arrangement has been made between the RBGE and the Forestry Commission, under which an area will be set aside in the forest of Glenbranter for the trial of exotic trees and shrubs'.

Glenbranter is located on the north-west shore of Loch Eck on the Cowal peninsula, in Argyll and Bute. The sheltered glen attracts heavy rainfall and little frost. A high canopy of native oak trees protected the proposed 50-acre planting site flanking the gorge beyond Glenbranter House [fig.5]. However,

Fig.5 | *Glenbranter House and Camp c.1935. Private collection.*

Fig.6 | *Benmore Forestry School with environs from high slopes above Rashfield, valley of Eachaig in mid-distance, 1932. Robert Moyes Adam. Photo: image (RMA-H2841) reproduced courtesy of St Andrews University Library Archive*

the retirement of Bayley Balfour in July 1922 placed the future of the Glenbranter project in the hands of his successor, William Wright Smith. It fell to Wright Smith to convince the Office of Works that the expense involved would not prove too onerous. Support came from *The Gardeners' Chronicle* which in December 1923 published an illustrated article including an endorsement of the project by 'Sir Isaac's old pupil Mr. George Forrest, whose epoch-making pioneer work in western China will pervade Glenbranter with material for years to come'. The feature dedicated the Glenbranter plantings as the Bayley Balfour Memorial Garden.

By December 1922 shipments of plants were arriving at Glenbranter via Kilmun, as detailed in early dispatch books kept at RBGE. This was the start of the great west coast

Rhododendron garden envisaged by Bayley Balfour – one that would ultimately be realised on another site. In addition to planting, plans regarding the design and construction of a dedicated memorial to Sir Isaac Bayley Balfour at Glenbranter appear to have been discussed prior to the following announcement within the pages of *The Transactions of the Royal Scottish Arboricultural Society*:

… it is suggested that the Memorial to Sir Isaac should take the form of a rest-house for the use of visitors. This might consist of a simple shelter designed by a good architect, or possibly, if sufficient funds were forthcoming, of a somewhat larger building. Other adjuncts such as an entrance gate or bridge over the burn might be considered.

The entry concluded by inviting subscriptions before listing members of a small executive committee as Sir John Stirling Maxwell, Pollok House; Professor W Wright Smith, RBGE; Mr Frederick Robert Stephen Balfour (1873–1945), Dawyck; and acting as Honorary Secretary and Treasurer, Mr John D. Sutherland, 25 Drumsheugh Gardens, Edinburgh. The public appeal also appeared within the pages of *The Gardeners' Chronicle* which noted that by December 1923 financial support amounting to £600 had reached the committee. A well-presented four-page brochure featuring an extended General Committee of 32 members was prepared and circulated outlining the plans and inviting donations [see Appendix]. A Statement of Account dated 5 November 1923 notes personal contributions and pledges ranging from 10 shillings to £100, with the Royal Horticultural Society promising a sum of £105.

Benmore and a Change of Direction

While the early planting at Glenbranter was underway and fundraising activities for the memorial shelter gathered pace, events elsewhere presented the possibility of an alternative site for consideration. Members of the memorial fund executive committee attending a meeting on 14 November 1924 were alerted to the availability of Benmore, some eight miles south of Glenbranter, and to the potential of acquiring part of the old wood there. The session closed with general concurrence that the garden might well be transferred to that place.

Benmore Estate [fig.6] had benefited from tree-planting activity dating back to 1820. In 1861 the estate was purchased by wealthy Scots-American James Piers Patrick (1818–85). He made many improvements at Benmore but is best remembered for planting the avenue of giant redwoods which grace the entrance to the garden. Between the years of 1871 and 1881 the innovative proprietor James Duncan (1834–1905) drained and fenced large areas of land at Benmore prior to planting six and a half million trees within an area totalling 1,622 acres. This undertaking demonstrates a major achievement and confirms Duncan

Fig.7 | *Overseas guests at Benmore House in the aftermath of the Royal Scottish Arboricultural Society Diamond Jubilee celebrations, July 1914. Photograph by Harry George Younger. Image reproduced courtesy of Royal Scottish Forestry Society.*

as an important player in the development of
scientific forestry in Scotland. It is intriguing
to note that in November 1875 James Duncan
attended the annual meeting of the Royal
Scottish Arboricultural Society at RBGE in
Edinburgh. It was Sir Isaac Bayley Balfour's
father, John Hutton Balfour, who, as Society
President, delivered the main address. Later,
in July 1914, Benmore played host to overseas dignitaries [fig.7] in the aftermath of
the Royal Scottish Arboricultural Society's
Diamond Jubilee celebrations.

The Youngers at Benmore

The liveried ale-carts advertising William
Younger & Co. Ltd must have been a familiar
sight all over Scotland by the time Henry
John Younger (1832–1913) purchased the
combined estates of Benmore, Bernice and
Kilmun in late 1889. The family brewing
business, established in 1778 within the
precincts of the Abbey of Holyrood House,
had expanded through the decades to develop
lucrative domestic and overseas markets.
Private clients included the Tsar and his
household in St Petersburg who are said to
have enjoyed an extra-strong Younger brew.

Younger paid £110,237 for what the
estate agent's sale brochure deemed the
'Magnificent Highland Domain of Benmore'
and ran the estate primarily to satisfy his
sporting interests. It is he who is credited with
introducing the first *Rhododendron* plantings
to Benmore. He was succeeded in 1913 by his
son Harry George Younger (1866–1951) who
took a close interest in the woods at Benmore
and continued with the pioneering reforestation work commenced by James Duncan.
Harry George Younger was also a keen horticulturist and developed a collection of rare
ornamental flowering trees and shrubs.

However, changed social attitudes and
economic constraints in the aftermath of
World War I proved a watershed for many

private estates in Scotland, and by 1924 the
cost of running Benmore was proving a serious
financial burden.

Gifting of Benmore

The *Glasgow Herald* of 13 February 1925
featured an article announcing the intention
of Harry George Younger to gift his estates
of 11,000 acres to the nation for afforestation
purposes. Proposals included education in
silviculture and the development of a National
Arboretum and Botanical Garden. The Forestry
Commission adapted Benmore House [fig.8] t
become a place of forestry instruction:

[Forming] *two sections, one of which is assigned to a school for working forest apprentices* [with] *the main section reserved as a Hostel for the reception of members of any University Senatus, lecturers, graduates or students in Botany or Forestry or allied sciences.*

Kilmun was identified as the preferred site to accommodate a forest garden project or collection of trial plots. In 1930 the Forestry Commission commenced work, setting aside some 250 acres on the hillside above the Holy Loch for small blocks of as many species of forest trees as could be made available. When intimation of Younger's gift was made public, the Royal Scottish Arboricultural Society nominated him as an Honorary Member for services to forestry. Legislative formalities appear customarily measured and deliberate with the Register for Sasines applicable to the County of Argyll formally recognising on 12 November 1925 the Deed of Gift enacted on 29 July 1925.

MY DEAR FORREST

In the winter of 1924–5 George Forrest was recuperating at Tengchong between collecting trips in Western Yunnan. In February, Wright Smith wrote:

My Dear Forrest, I have great news ... Mr Harry Younger has presented his estate of Benmore ... into the keeping of The Forestry Commission with the exception of such areas as I may like to choose for a Rhododendron area. Now this area you probably know. It is on the way to Glenbranter and only 3 or 4 miles from the pier [at Kilmun]. You will no doubt remember the magnificent avenue of conifers and the huge banks of vegetation round the entrance gates to Benmore.

A month later Wright Smith dispatched a further letter:

My Dear Forrest, I think it is pretty well agreed that the estate at Benmore will afford much better facilities than Glenbranter. When you are home again and have an opportunity of seeing Benmore I am quite sure that you will approve of the choice.

Younger Botanic Garden Benmore

William Wright Smith visited Benmore at the earliest opportunity. He wrote to Sir Lionel Earle (1866–1948) at the Office of Works on 9 March 1925:

Mr Younger's donation has taken the Forestry Commission as well as ourselves by surprise ... It is a munificent gift ... The position of Benmore persuades me strongly that it will be most advantageous to make it the centre of the Memorial Rhododendron Garden instead of Glenbranter.

Subsequently, memorial fund secretary and treasurer John D. Sutherland contacted Wright Smith in the summer of 1925 advising a temporary delay to plans regarding the proposed rest house or shelter. He wrote: 'I saw Sir John Maxwell yesterday and have also seen Mr Younger. It is suggested that we should defer a meeting until we can all get to Benmore sometime early September'.

Developments were gathering pace with the first documented consignment of plants from RBGE arriving at Benmore in 1925. However, the formal gifting of Benmore was a protracted affair and Younger did not completely hand over his estate until towards the end of 1928. The policies surrounding Benmore House became the 90-acre Younger Botanic Garden (Benmore) under the guidance of Regius Keeper William Wright Smith. This arrangement was welcomed by many horticulturists including tree enthusiast and memorial fund executive committee member F.R.S. Balfour of Dawyck who wrote of Benmore in *The Rhododendron Society Notes* that:

Professor W. Wright Smith and his able coadjutors ... are greatly to be envied in having such a venue available for the contents of their Edinburgh frames and seed pans ... it would be almost impossible to find in Scotland an area better suited to the growing of Rhododendrons and most conifers.

Puck's Glen

Sir Isaac Bayley Balfour Memorial Rest House Location Revealed

On 6 October 1925 John D. Sutherland wrote to William Wright Smith identifying Puck's Glen [fig.9] as the permanent location for the planned tribute to the memory of Sir Isaac Bayley Balfour. It was separated from Benmore House and its policies by the main road. All parties, including Harry George Younger and the Office of Works, agreed that:

The Bayley Balfour Memorial Trustees will erect a Rest House or Shelter as a Memorial to Sir Isaac Bayley Balfour on the site mutually selected. The Rest House or Shelter when finished will be handed over to The Forestry Commission [who will] *become responsible for the proper maintenance of the building and furnishings.*

F.R.S. Balfour revealed the decision on the siting to the Rhododendron Society, writing 'a more picturesque place it would be difficult to imagine'.

Eas Mor or Uig Glen (Puck's Glen)

Cartographers working on the Ordnance Survey First Edition (1869) series at a scale of 6 inch to 1 mile struggled to represent accurately the narrowness and enclosure of the Argyllshire gorge known locally as Eas Mor – even on modern maps the gorge on the steep broken hillside remains elusive.

An early reference to the location is recorded within the Minute Book of the Greenock Natural History Society. Members had planned an excursion, with the permission of landowner James Duncan, to Uig Glen on 22 May 1880 and enjoyed an extended stay, delaying their departure from Kilmun until early evening. The entry provides a useful description and summary of the site:

Uig Glen was entered upon from the public road and had been made accessible by a path cut along its precipitous banks, while it abounded in wild flowers and the addition of cultivated varieties distributed with taste. The following is a list of a few of the wild plants met with viz.: – Anemome nemorosa, Stellaria holostea *(in great profusion),* Sanicula europaea, Pinguicula vulgaris *(an insectivorous plant),* Anchusa sempervirens – a rather rare plant. Melica uniflora *(a very pretty grass) and a number of the common ferns.*

The strata of the glen consisted of schist rocks, in some instances highly impregnated with peroxide of iron, and pretty much contorted, the only igneous rock observed being a trap dyke of a black colour and very much disintegrated.

A contemporary review of *The Plantations of the Estates of Benmore and Kilmun* (1883) confirms recently implemented initiatives to improve access within the policies. Forester Donald Stalker described the Uig and Rashfield plantations (which include the Eas Mor waterfall):

On this part of the estate ... which contributes in no small measure to its attractions

... a bridle path, five feet wide ... has lately been constructed, at a cost of 2s. per lineal yard, including wooden bridges which span the burns ... between huge overhanging rocks, in the crevices and sides of which are an endless variety of ferns, mosses, and other Alpine plants, the burn flows rapidly down in a series of waterfalls.

By 1889 the deep narrow ravine was described as 'fully 2 miles long ... at every turn of the path a new prospect is opened up. The stream is crossed by several rustic bridges ... seats are provided at the most convenient and picturesque spots'.

However, these descriptions do little to prepare visitors for the heightened experience awaiting in Puck's Glen.

Sprites and Fairies within Traditional Scottish Folklore

Traditional Scottish folklore has had a long and sometimes wary relationship with sprites and fairies and the ghostlike netherworlds they inhabit. In 1815 Sir Walter Scott (1771–1832) released *The Secret Commonwealth* based on previously unpublished papers. The book provides insight into the clandestine activities of a myriad of phantasmal creatures and beings. The source material was a manuscript written by respected Episcopalian minister Robert Kirk (1644–92) of Aberfoyle in Perthshire. Following his revelations and alleged betrayal of the secrets of 'the wee folk' Kirk suffered an early and unexplained death.

Puck is identifiable as a specific 16th-century malicious spirit or demon of popular superstition. With older links claimed to both Teutonic and Celtic language traditions the origin of the name is otherwise uncertain. Puck, also known as Robin Goodfellow or Hobgoblin, gained recognition and wider infamy as the impish trickster in Shakespeare's *A Midsummer Night's Dream* (written 1595/6) and is often portrayed visually as a form of the Greek god Pan.

The Naming of Puck's Glen by William (Crimea) Simpson

Glasgow-born artist and war correspondent William (Crimea) Simpson (1823–99) was convalescing at Kilmun in the autumn of 1857. A ghostly or ethereal fixation within popular Victorian culture, together with a sometimes unshakeable willingness to believe in the existence of sprites and fairies, perhaps influenced Simpson. He sensed the presence of a mischievous temperament within the enchanted fairyland of Eas Mor. Drawing upon rich seams of folklore and cultural reference Simpson renamed the gorge Puck's Glen. It was here, on a level platform overlooking this 'scene of the wildest grandeur ... innumerable cataracts filling the air with the pleasant music of falling water', that Sir Robert Lorimer chose to locate the Sir Isaac Bayley Balfour Memorial Rest House.

Fig.9 | *Postcard view of Puck's Glen, undated. Private collection.*

The Architect, Contractor and Sculptor

The Architect: Sir Robert Lorimer

It is unlikely that the 'good architect' nominated by Sir John Stirling Maxwell would be anyone other than the trusted and highly experienced Sir Robert Lorimer (1864–1929). The men were close associates for a period of 20 years and shared many common interests. A disciple of the Arts and Crafts movement, Lorimer [fig.10] adapted early Scots Baronial traditions to create his own distinctive style of architecture. Major residential commissions included Earlshall (1892), Rowallan (1902), Wemyss Hall (1905), since renamed Hill of Tarvit, and Ardkinglas (1906). The prolific Lorimer is recognised as being responsible for the creation of 'a new kind of design for Scotland based on his own passion for materials and craft'.

Lorimer's abilities extended to the principles and practice of garden design, for instance as part of the extensive remodelling of the Formakin estate in Renfrewshire for stockbroker John Holms (1866–1938). Lorimer was an associate of contemporaries such as the architect Sir Edwin Lutyens (1869–1944) and an occasional collaborator with Gertrude Jekyll (1843–1932), whom he described as 'a great authority on gardening and arts and crafts, and a great character generally'. Closer to home the modest garden belonging to Miss Frances Hope (1822–80) at Wardie Lodge in Edinburgh, together with her posthumously published writings, specifically *Notes & Thoughts on Gardens & Woodlands* (1881), have been credited as a major source of inspiration to the architect. Lorimer would also renew his creative energy

Fig.10 | *Sir Robert Lorimer (1864–1929) by John M. Aiken (1880–1961).*
Image reproduced courtesy of Royal Incorporation of Architects in Scotland.

by returning to his early work laid out for his mother and father within the enclosed wall garden at Kellie Castle in Fife. By the mid-1920s Sir Robert Lorimer's reputation as the national architect of Scotland was established.

Lorimer and Homegrown Timber

A lesser-known aspect of Sir Robert Lorimer's career was his involvement with the movement to promote the supply and use of homegrown timber within Scotland. His paper entitled 'The Neglect of Home Timber' appeared in *Country Life* magazine in April 1916 and was reproduced verbatim within the pages of *Transactions of the Royal Scottish Arboricultural Society*. In the article Lorimer shares his knowledge on the best use of the many different timbers already growing in Scotland, for example:

The indigenous Scots Pine ... if carefully selected makes beautiful panelling. Many old Scottish houses contain charming rooms, such as the well-known room at Rosslyn Castle, panelled in red Pine, untouched by either paint or varnish, which time has turned into a beautiful cool colour.

However, in concluding a toast to his hosts at a Royal Scottish Arboricultural Society annual dinner he urged members 'not to confine their activities to the production of soft timbers because there were no more beautiful woods in the world than Scottish hardwoods'. The aesthete and craftsman in Lorimer burned brightly.

A practical application of his understanding of homegrown timber was Lorimer's commission to design the purpose-built timber 'village hall' display by the Royal Scottish Arboricultural Society at the 1924 British Empire Exhibition [fig.11]. Constructed by Messrs William Black & Sons of Brechin, the exhibit showcased the quality and value of a range of Scottish-grown timbers. Scots pine provided the frame of

Fig.11 | *Lorimer's Timber Village Hall at British Empire Exhibition 1924. Image reproduced courtesy of Royal Scottish Forestry Society.*

Fig.12 | *Postcard view of the road through Benmore estate leading to Puck's Glen, c.1900. Private collection.*

the building and waney-edged elm the lower weatherboarding. Oak was used for the pillars, with creosoted Scots pine shingles covering the roof. The interior was lined with samples of 'several kinds of coniferous timbers to show their respective appearances in this class of work'. Lorimer would adapt some of these details for the Sir Isaac Bayley Balfour Memorial Rest House.

Design of Puck's Hut

Sir Robert Lorimer liked to quote prominent Arts and Crafts designer William Morris (1834–96) who advocated 'if you have a building to put up in a countryside go to the place ... use all the local materials and ways of doing things as far as you can'. Correspondence dated 23 June 1926 records that John D. Sutherland hoped to join Sir John Stirling Maxwell and Lorimer on a planned trip to Benmore [fig.12]. Although Lorimer's reaction to Puck's Glen has not been recorded the sheer spectacle and drama of its natural setting must have had an influence on both the siting of his building and its design.

The idea of a memorial rest house at Glenbranter had been suggested as far back as 1923. If there was an extended written design brief for the project, it has not survived. Lorimer's creative ability would have been trusted, perhaps subject to cursory approval. Lorimer designed an oak-framed octagonal building set on a dais of locally hewn stone. The structure featured a bell-shaped shingle roof, multi-pane casement windows on four sides, a partially glazed two-leaf entrance door and a stone-built chimney. Details included an internal fireplace, a carved stone dedication tablet and roof apex carved figure. Forging a meaningful link with the living landscape, wherever possible locally grown timber from the Benmore estate would be cut and seasoned for use. Site inaccessibility

would also have influenced the selection of construction materials. Timber would permit some workshop preparation and ease transport complications.

Architectural roof work associated with Lorimer has a consistent and distinct appearance, very often based upon various combinations of hips and valleys. Editor and architectural reviewer Walter Shaw Sparrow (1862–1940) wrote perceptively of the natural environment informing this aspect of Lorimer's work. He noted:

the very first quality to be shown is unity of impression. Dame Nature has always that quality in her coned fungi and domed mushrooms and I cannot help but thinking that the present-day masters of roof construction like E L Lutyens and Mr Lorimer have taken hints from nature's art in coverlids.

Whether intended by Lorimer or otherwise this conspicuous design trait found perfect expression within Puck's Glen.

By the mid-1920s Lorimer had surrounded himself with a number of experienced and trusted craftsmen who understood his long-established methods and working practice. In dealing with his operatives, Lorimer felt that 'an architect should regard himself as the conductor of an orchestra'. Lorimer had long championed a national style of craftsmanship across many disciplines. By providing encouragement and careful patronage 'he had [effectively] trained a body of workers in all the crafts to a perfect sense of the character of distinctively Scottish work'.

From c.1913 Lorimer worked from 17 Great Stuart Street, Edinburgh. In 1927 his office manager (and first apprentice) John Matthew (1875–1955) was assumed into partnership and the practice renamed Lorimer & Matthew. It is almost certain that Matthew oversaw drawings prepared for the Sir Isaac

Bayley Balfour Memorial Rest House. Upon completion of a project, drawings were stored in the basement, or as one commentator recalled: 'abandoned might be a better word, they were piled on the floor and stacked up until they reached knee height'. While much excellent work has since been undertaken to conserve the considerable Lorimer archive, extensive searches across many public collections have not identified any original drawings associated with the Sir Isaac Bayley Balfour Memorial Rest House. At present the drawings, if they have survived, remain unlocated.

The Contractor: Scott Morton & Tynecastle Co. Ltd

The Edinburgh-based family business of Scott Morton & Tynecastle Co. Ltd had emerged in 1920 from older companies founded by Lanarkshire-born architect, artist, craftsman and decorator William Scott Morton (1840–1903). Leading designers and producers of quality interior woodwork and furniture, Scott Morton & Co. dressed, wholly or partially, country houses as well as working under the supervision of eminent architects of the time. In the closing decades of the 19th century Scott Morton & Co. were one of two firms that executed most of Lorimer's joinery and architectural woodwork. By the time the design of Puck's Hut was on the drawing board the company was Lorimer's first choice for skilled carpentry and woodcraft. As nominated contractor, Scott Morton returned drawings to Lorimer on 18 May 1927. The attached covering letter estimated a probable cost of £520 for woodwork and erection of the Memorial to Sir Isaac Bayley Balfour at Benmore, Dunoon. The surviving Scott Morton & Co. job book located within Historic Environment Scotland archives lists the order as number 555.

Selection of Materials

The framework of the building is made from oak. It is possible to work out other original construction details from correspondence associated with the project. Larch was proposed for roof timbers, with elm suggested for weatherboard cladding. The ceiling lining was also to be made of oak. Lorimer sought advice on the roof shingles from Nathaniel Grieve of Edinburgh, who recommended that 'a good quality felt should be put under the shingles and these should be copper nailed to the roof boarding by a competent tradesman'. The Forestry Commission eventually supplied timber for the roof shingles. Western red cedar logs were sent via Strone to A & G Paterson Ltd at St Rollox Sawmills Glasgow and a quantity of 3,700 seasoned and creosoted tiles were returned to Kilmun in February 1927. Freight and service charges amounted to £33 11s 9d to which John D. Sutherland wrote to remind Lorimer 'the value of the timber will have to be added'. The interior panels representing many of the timbers growing at Benmore are an attractive and popular feature of the Sir Isaac Bayley Balfour Memorial Rest House, and Sutherland informed the architect:

We are arranging to have panels of Sitka Spruce, Douglas Fir, European Larch, Thuja, Abies nobilis, Scots Pine, Norway Spruce, Abies grandis, Tsuga mertensiana, Sequoia gigantea and possibly Lawson Cypress, cut and seasoned for the Rest House. It has been suggested that the remaining nine panels might be made up of Oak, Ash, Elm, Beech, Sycamore, Cherry, Birch, Poplar and Willow.

The ever-reliable Sutherland applied his practical knowledge of forestry and timber by expressing some anxiety regarding the short time available for seasoning and dressing, and proposed 'that the panels might be fitted so

Fig.13 | *Sir Isaac Bayley Balfour Memorial Rest House, interior hearth and fireplace with memorial tablet, 1930. Robert Moyes Adam. Photo: image (RMA-H2337) reproduced courtesy of St Andrews University Library Archive.*

that they could later be removed and replaced by better examples should this be found necessary'.

Workshop Construction, Logistics and Onsite Construction

Scott Morton & Co. Ltd workshops were located on Murieston Road in Edinburgh. Machine shop time, joiners and apprentice rates were all charged to the project. The inventory of materials listed a supply of

timber at a cost of £108 3s 8d with fixings (including a galvanised hoop) totalling £7 3s 1d. Component parts were carefully marked, wrapped and packed into transporting crates in preparation for the journey westwards. Expenses incurred included pier dues, hires and railway carriages. To build the memorial onsite, Scott Morton sent a foreman joiner and accompanying ordinary joiner who each claimed 298 hours, 'out time with country allowance'.

Gaining access to the proposed memorial site was problematic. The bridle path by the burn, constructed in the 1870s by James Duncan, had deteriorated and was now incomplete. Benmore estate factor John Webster recounted that 'the majority of rustic bridges got into a state of disrepair and as a precautionary measure it was decided to demolish them ... the walk through the ravine can only be accomplished when the stream is low'. Lorimer was aware of the situation and no doubt thought he was being helpful by suggesting 'as the hut is at the top of the glen there is no method of transport except carrying the stuff on the back of a pony or mule'. Despite these difficulties, eventually everything was in place and the work was completed by the end of 1927.

Puck's Hut on its Original Site

A woodland clearing above the glen offered a level platform as an obvious setting for the building. The location required visitors to emerge from the steep-sided ravine to seek refuge within the shelter. Lorimer took full advantage of the elevated site by positioning the windows to look north-west across the tree-tops to A' Cruach and Bhein Mohr beyond.

Sir Robert Lorimer described himself as an 'enthusiast of wood fires', sharing his passion and knowledge of the subject in an article published in *The Times* on 9 January 1929. He also had an open fire in his Edinburgh office where 'he liked to burn wood and he so liked its smell that he'd take a glowing log and swing it round and round to scent the air'. A prominent design feature of the Sir Isaac Bayley Balfour Memorial Rest House in its original location was the internal fireplace [fig.13]. This inspired detail from Lorimer, invoking thoughts of a warm cosy cabin, the lure of wood smoke drifting lazily through the forest, must have helped entice visitors to the hut. The accompanying stone-built chimney stack added a certain degree of lopsided eccentricity to the external appearance of the building and was constructed at a cost of £135 by subcontractors Messrs Neil McLeod & Sons of Edinburgh.

The Sculptor: Phyllis Bone ARSA

Sir Robert Lorimer had a long tradition of decorating his buildings with grotesques. The location of the Bayley Balfour Memorial demanded a Puck-like figure to overlook the glen. He asked animal sculptor Phyllis Mary Bone (1894–1972), with whom he had worked previously on the Scottish National War Memorial at Edinburgh Castle, to create a figure to adorn the roof apex of the rest house. Working from her studio at 5 Alva Street in Edinburgh, Bone prepared a preparatory plaster model of a satyr, complete with cloven hooves, cradling a lamb; an accompanying red squirrel provided further detail. The maquette (including an invoice for £23 10s) was forwarded to wood carvers employed by Scott Morton & Co. Ltd and was later displayed at the 1928 Annual Exhibition of the Royal Scottish Academy.

Scott Morton & Co. charged 136 hours' workshop time for woodcarving associated with the memorial project. These hours presumably included time to create the carved wooden finial, using the plaster model as a template, which added much value and imaginative expression to the memorial shelter [fig.14].

Arcadia in Argyll

Phyllis Bone named her creation Pan. While she was unquestionably the energetic force that produced a highly detailed and distinctive artefact, Sir Robert Lorimer's gentle prompting and offstage direction is unmistakeable. The Ancient Greeks celebrated Pan as the god of shepherds, flocks and wooded glens. Pan, with his crown of leaves and the horns, legs and hindquarters of a goat, could only be worshipped in open settings, hence

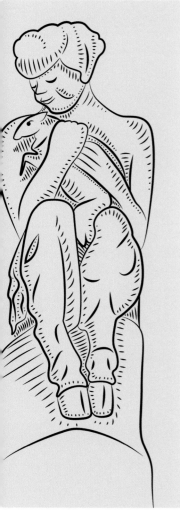

Fig.14 | *Pan by Phyllis Mary Bone. Weathered (c.2005), an artist's impression (c.2015) and storm damaged (c.2010). Photographs by Peter Baxter. Original artwork by Shirley Lochhead.*

his association with wilderness or rustic Arcadia. In practical garden design work Lorimer rarely strayed from his stated preferences which included traditional elements of formality, walled enclosures, balustraded terraces and garden pavilions. He saw gardens as 'a sort of sanctuary ... a chamber roofed by heaven to wander in, to cherish, to dream through undisturbed, a little pleasuance by whose wicket the world can be shut'. He did,

however, concede a contrasting viewpoint by revealing a fondness for ornamenting remoter parts of the wild garden with 'some woodland deity, half smothered in honeysuckle or the wild rose'. Puck's Glen offered the most natural and dramatic of woodland settings. The selection of Pan as the carved finial topping the Sir Isaac Bayley Balfour Memorial Rest House allowed Lorimer to deliver a vision or interpretation of Arcadia in Argyll.

Charles d'Orville Pilkington Jackson
ARSA, FRBS, FRSA

Charles d'Orville Pilkington Jackson (1887–1973) was another of the many craftsmen Lorimer could rely upon. They had formed a strong relationship working together on the Scottish National War Memorial. Pilkington Jackson's reputation as a talented carver and sculptor had flourished thanks to this project. Lorimer confirmed in a letter dated 27 February 1928 that 'this octagon-shaped hut was recently erected as a memorial to Sir Isaac Bayley Balfour. A panel 24 inch square or thereby including the moulding is required to be inserted above the chimney piece'. Lorimer closed by dictating the proposed inscription, including pencilled last-minute changes, and requesting 'would you get your man to rough it out in old Scotch lettering of the usual type'.

Regius Keeper William Wright Smith drafted an inscription to be included within the Puck's Glen memorial. While objecting to the inclusion of the word 'hut' he eventually gave way to 'a very much superior' dedication proposed by Sir John Stirling Maxwell. Pilkington Jackson supplied and carved the memorial panel [fig.15] 'containing one hundred and two letters in Doddington Stone for £18 packed on rail'. Stirling Maxwell's inscription, amended by Lorimer, read:

> THIS HUT AND GLEN ARE DEDICATED
> BY HIS FRIENDS TO THE MEMORY OF SIR
> ISAAC BAYLEY BALFOUR IN FULFILMENT
> OF A PLAN HE CHERISHED

Harry George Younger's Tribute to James Duncan

Harry George Younger's father had purchased the estate of Benmore and Kilmun in 1889 from James Duncan, and Younger took it upon himself to include a small tribute to the former Laird of Benmore within the soon to be dedicated Sir Isaac Bayley Balfour Memorial Rest

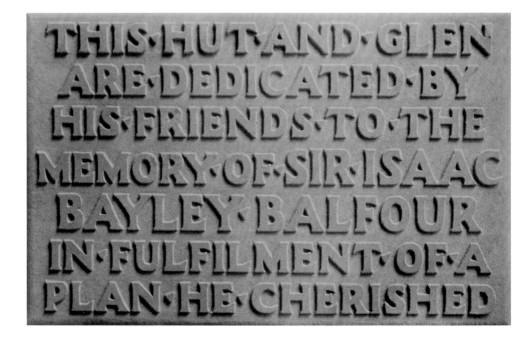

Fig.15 | *Detail of Sir Isaac Bayley Balfour Memorial Rest House carved dedication tablet. Pilkington Jackson. Image (ACC 8542–19–29) reproduced courtesy of National Library of Scotland.*

Fig.16 | *Harry George Younger's carved tribute to James Duncan. Photograph by Sybil Gray ,2020.*

House. After Younger had called Sir Robert Lorimer regarding an additional carved panel, the architect forwarded to Scott Morton & Co. the following inscription with the instruction that the bill be sent to Mr Younger:

> REMEMBER JAMES DUNCAN WHO HAD
> THE FORESIGHT AND COURAGE TO
> ORIGINATE THE PLANTING WHICH
> CLOTHED THESE HILLS AND GLENS WITH
> THE WOODS YOU NOW ENJOY

Scott Morton & Co. estimated a sum of £10 16s 'to furnish material, make and deliver [to] Dunoon, carved, lettered and decorated memorial tablet to drawing'. The surviving 25 × 10 inch tablet is made of oak with low-relief characters set against a red painted background. Tiny carved rosettes provide further detail along the top edge. The memorial plaque is set within a mitred dark timber moulding, which may have been added later. Lorimer pledged 'when I go to inspect the job I must examine the available space above the chimneypiece with the view to working this in'. Keeping his word, Lorimer visited the construction site on 25 November 1927. Disembarking at Kirn in the company of Sir John Stirling Maxwell and William Wright Smith, the threesome travelled to Puck's Glen by pre-arranged motor. In terms of development at Benmore, James Duncan

is more than worthy of his place alongside Sir Isaac Bayley Balfour. It is a simple and thoughtful tribute [fig.16].

Final Building Certificate

The invoice dated 26 December 1927 [fig.17] is costed at £603 4s 10d, and the final building certificate, dated 11 January 1928, for the Shelter at Benmore, Dunoon, names Colonel J. Sutherland as the client. Lorimer discounted £5 from his design and consultancy fee of £60.

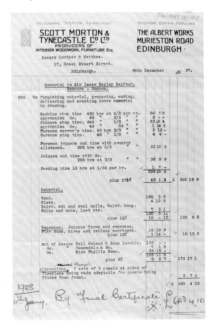

Fig.17 | *Scott Morton & Co. Ltd typewritten invoice in respect of Bayley Balfour Memorial, Benmore, Dunoon, dated 26 December 1927. Image reproduced courtesy of Edinburgh University Library Research Collections.*

Opening

Robert Moyes Adam

Robert Moyes Adam (1885–1967) started work at RBGE in 1903 preparing lecture illustrations for Sir Isaac Bayley Balfour. In 1915 he was promoted to the newly created post of Photographer and Artist. Over a period of 35 years he gained a reputation as one of the country's foremost landscape photographers, illustrating publications such as *The Highlands of Scotland* (1936) and *The Scots Magazine*. As an insightful reviewer of his archive has noted: 'many of Adam's images constitute a pictorial lament for a Scotland all but lost to us now'.

Moyes Adam visited Puck's Glen on 12 March 1928. Always working in monochrome, he took the first known picture of the Sir Isaac Bayley Balfour Memorial Rest House [fig.18]. This early image demonstrates a considerable talent and provides an invaluable site record. Moyes Adam was also responsible for the only known surviving interior shot [fig.13] of the rest house. Standing in the foreground of the external image by Moyes Adam are four figures and a dog. On the extreme left is John White (1889–1943). RBGE Service Roll and Employment Records note that White joined as a probationer in December 1912 before enlisting in the 9th Royal Scots two years later. Demobilised in 1919, he completed his final trainee year at RBGE before attaining the position of Head Gardener to Harry George Younger at Benmore. White progressed to the role of RBGE Curator at Benmore. The pipe-smoking middle figures are Mr Hornby (Assistant Estate Factor) and John Webster (Estate Factor), presumably appointed to their respective positions by Younger. On the extreme right of the photograph is Kirriemuir-born Laurence Baxter Stewart (1877–1934). Baxter Stewart joined the staff of RBGE in 1901 and was referred to by Sir Isaac as 'the enthusiastic plant propagator whom I am so fortunate to have on my staff'. In 1915, at the age of 38, Baxter Stewart decided to enlist. Bayley Balfour hushed the anxieties of his concerned colleagues while defending the resolve of his propagator: 'Stewart, who is a crack rifle shot and a splendid cyclist and motor-cyclist ... [is] an extremely fit man for the army work'. It is a moment of sweet alchemy that many of the early accessions planted at Benmore would have been raised by Baxter Stewart upon his return.

Invitations to the Opening Ceremony

John D. Sutherland wrote personally to inform Sir Robert Lorimer that the formal opening of the memorial would take place on 8 September 1928. Travel arrangements and details of a special excursion were included within printed invitations sent out to other guests:

The train leaving Glasgow (St. Enoch Station) at 9.24 A.M. will reach Greenock (10.27 A.M.) in time to catch the Steamer which is due to arrive at Kilmun Pier at 11.45 A.M. Puck's Glen is about 2 miles from Kilmun. Charabanc facilities will be available from the pier to Puck's Glen.

Fig.18 | *Sir Isaac Bayley Balfour Memorial Rest House, Puck's Glen, 12 March 1928. Photograph by Robert Moyes Adam. Miscellaneous photographs in Benmore Curator's Office. Kindly made available by Peter Baxter.*

The publication of an illustrated 12-page commemorative brochure, including text prepared by novelist and journalist Neil Munro (1863–1930), coincided with the planned dedication service. Munro was born at nearby Inveraray and was fully immersed in the language and tradition of Gaelic culture. His early historical novels, such as *John Splendid* (1898) and *Doom Castle* (1901), as well as the lighter *Collected Stories from The Vital Spark* (1906), are set in and around Argyll. Throughout these works local scenery provides a constant and colourful backdrop and upon occasion Munro's descriptive skill elevates the power of the landscape 'that it becomes almost a protagonist in the tale'. The booklet, printed by R & R Clark Ltd of Edinburgh, featured six uncredited black and white images contributed by Robert Moyes Adam.

Dedication of the Sir Isaac Bayley Balfour Memorial Rest House

The ceremony was scheduled to commence at 12.30 p.m. and to be undertaken by Sir Herbert Maxwell, who two years earlier had performed a similar task at RBGE. An affable individual, Maxwell was at this time amongst the best-known public figures in Scotland. A grand old man of politics, books and letters, he had a wide range of interests and was in possession of a comprehensive knowledge of all matters Scottish. His published titles included *Scottish Gardens* (1908) and *Trees – A Woodland Notebook* (1915).

A newspaper photograph [fig.19] and press articles reported spectator numbers swelled by a visit from the Botanical and Forestry section of the British Association that coincided with the event. *The Gardeners' Chronicle* of 8 September 1928 reproduced the comments of Neil Munro who described the spirit of the occasion in lavish terms:

It is to the memory of Bayley Balfour, his great personal charm and scientific genius, and his lifelong service to a science which is the ministrant to natural beauty, as much as to the utilitarian ideals of farmer and forester, that The Forestry Commission has dedicated the most charmingly poetical feature – Puck's Glen.

OPENING OF PUCK'S GLEN REST HUT

Fig.19 | *Opening of Puck's Glen Rest Hut*, The Bulletin, 10 September 1928. Image reproduced courtesy of RBGE Library & Archive Services.

Fig.20 | *Sir Isaac Bayley Balfour Memorial Rest House opening ceremony 8 September 1928. Photo: image (3516) reproduced courtesy of Forestry Memories (www.forestry-memories.org.uk).*

A photograph [fig.20] taken on the day captures the attendance of Harry George Younger; the botanist and mycologist Professor Dame Helen Gwynne Vaughan (1879–1967); Sir Herbert Maxwell; suitably equipped for the Argyll weather, former Director of Royal Botanic Gardens, Kew Sir David Prain (1857–1944); and William Wright Smith, RBGE Regius Keeper.

Rules and Regulations and Budgetary Concerns

William Wright Smith, referring to the 'Isaac Bayley Balfour Memorial Arboretum in Puck's Glen', drafted a basic outline of rules and regulations in respect of free admission to the public. The proposals included a no-liability statement and guidelines on suggested opening hours. It is difficult to understand why Wright Smith took it upon himself to become involved with site management. In respect of Puck's Glen the all-party agreement of October 1925 had made it clear that the entire works, with the exception of occasional supervising and conducting of horticultural operations by the Office of Works, would be undertaken at the cost of the Forestry Commission.

There is a hint of growing frustration at a perceived lack of resources to develop the policies immediately surrounding Benmore House. Having previously thought that relocation from Glenbranter to Benmore would not result in greater expenditure,

Wright Smith demonstrated considerable executive dexterity within a later memo, presumably to the Office of Works. He stated: 'the whole matter resolves into a question of labour. I believe that the labour charges for several years could be met completely by an additional charge of £300 per annum'.

The Younger (Benmore) Trust

The timing may be coincidental but it would appear that Harry George Younger took matters into his own hands to help reduce the burden of developing the recently gifted garden at Benmore. Younger, almost certainly guided by Sir John Stirling Maxwell, set up the Younger (Benmore) Trust whereby certain properties and superiorities were disponed in order to yield an annual return. Specific instruction stated that duties and rents were to be 'used by the Trustees for the maintenance of the amenity, utility and beauty of the policies and garden of Benmore House'. Sir John Stirling Maxwell, William Wright Smith, John D. Sutherland and Harry George Younger were signatories and original committee members of the newly created trust fund. The agreement was formally recorded within the General Register of Sasines on 17 July 1929. The Younger (Benmore) Trust continues to this day to support the garden.

The First Forty Years and the Moving of Puck's Hut

Fig.21 | *Postcard view of Puck's Glen entrance c.1935. Private collection.*

Popularity of Memorial, Argyll National Forest Park & Public Access

In the 1930s the free-spirited open-air or weekender movement began to occupy the countryside, with ramblers and hillwalkers taking to the great outdoors on a regular basis. Urban lowland workers and other city dwellers led the charge to escape from the industrial heartlands and economic depression. Rail and steamer services made crossing the River Clyde a relatively straightforward proposition with bus companies such as Dunoon Motor Services and Blackhams waiting at the pier head. This accessibility to public transport helped turn Argyll and the Cowal peninsula into a well-frequented destination with Puck's Glen and the memorial rest house encapsulating these new social trends. A car parking or drop-off area was created near the southern entrance to the glen with a robust rustic fence and decorative

gate added [fig.21]. Paths and footbridges must have been reinstated allowing access to Puck's Hut directly from the gorge. University of Glasgow Regius Professor of Botany John Walton (1895–1971) captured the appeal of the setting: 'not far from Benmore is Puck's Glen, a place of great natural charm, with the memorial hut to Sir Isaac Bayley Balfour on the hill above the tree-tops'.

In 1936, Puck's Glen was included within the boundary of the 58,000-acre Argyll National Forest Park, the first forest park created by the Forestry Commission in the United Kingdom. Chairman Sir Roy Lister Robinson (1883–1952) emphasised the provision of 'recreational facilities for those who love the Scottish mountains, forests and lochs' as the principal aim of the forest park initiative. Success was measured in terms of annual visits, which included 50,000 people using public camping grounds. Many others stayed in youth hostels at Ardgartan, Strone (Dunselma) and Inverbeg. A wide range of outdoor activities included boating and pony-trekking, with several sites recommended for cold-water sea bathing.

Early National Forest Park attempts to promote outdoor activity as a leisure pastime gained further impetus as a consequence of the Countryside Act (1968) and ultimately with the Land Reform (Scotland) Act (2003) granting everyone the right of responsible access over 'freedom to roam' land throughout Scotland. The commitment to promoting recreational enjoyment was further endorsed by an Act of Parliament that set up Loch Lomond & The Trossachs National Park. This overarching authority has encompassed the Argyll National Forest Park area since 2002 and is tasked with the aim of conserving and enhancing the natural and cultural heritage of the area.

Valentines of Dundee and Picture Postcard Views

The location in general and the Sir Isaac Bayley Balfour Memorial Rest House in particular proved to be popular attractions. The glen and Puck's Hut featured in many postcard views [figs 22–5], with a large number produced by Valentines of Dundee. Landscape photography and postcards in Scotland were for many decades synonymous with Valentines, originally founded in 1851 as a printing company by the pioneering James Valentine (1815–79). It was his business-savvy son and successor William Dobson Valentine (1844–1907) who made the shrewd decision to enter the picture postcard market. There is very little recorded information about photographers commissioned by the company but it is known that images were purchased from a wide variety of external photographers and agencies. The considerable Valentines archive of about 50,000 topographical views is located within the University of St Andrews Special Collections. It is an exceptional resource for many aspects of social history and helps provides us with contemporary photographs of Puck's Glen.

Fig.22 | *Postcard view of Puck's Hut, Puck's Glen, near Dunoon c.1935. Private collection.*

Fig.23 | *Postcard view of Sir Isaac Bayley Balfour Memorial Rest House, Puck's Glen c.1928. Private collection.*

Fig.24 | *Postcard view of Sir Isaac Bayley Balfour Memorial Rest House, Puck's Glen c.1940. Private collection.*

Fig.25 | *Postcard view of Puck's Glen footpath c.1935. Private collection.*

Relocation to Younger Botanic Garden

Puck's Hut stood for 40 years within the original location selected by Sir Robert Lorimer. By the mid-1960s there were concerns regarding the long-term security of the building. A decision was made by the Younger (Benmore) Trust in the summer of 1967 to obtain estimates for the cost of removal and re-erection of the memorial rest house. On 9 October 1967 estate factor K.A.H. Cassels (1919–2018) authorised on behalf of the Younger (Benmore) Trustees the relocation of the memorial to an unspecified site within the gardens at Benmore. The sum of £488 was accepted as an estimate of cost.

Jackson and Kay – Joiners and Builders

Proprietor William S. Kelly (1917–2015) of Jackson and Kay at 26 Hillfoot Street in

Dunoon anticipated that the relocation would not be straightforward. He informed Cassels 'this hut is not sectional and will be practically taken down piece by piece'.

Kelly secured agreement from Cassels that 'removal from the top of Puck's Glen and transport to Benmore will be supplied by you'. It appears that a decision had also been made not to relocate the stone-built chimney stack. The estimate by Kelly stated that 'one of the octagonal sides, where existing fireplace is, will be replaced with oak double doors or windows to match existing sides'. Further changes around this time appear to include a coat of dark preservative which masked the contrasting natural tones of the external panelling. It is also highly probable that some of the other exposed timber parts, such as the bearers, were replaced at this time. Cassels also asked Kelly to source oak shingles for the roof. It was incorrectly thought that the

Fig.26 [opposite] | *Sir Isaac Bayley Balfour Memorial Rest House relocated to the Walled Garden at RBGE Benmore c.1980. Photograph by Don MacCaskill (courtesy of Bridget MacCaskill, Strathyre).*

original shingles fitted by Scott Morton & Co. in the 1920s were larch. The expense of oak shingles ultimately proved too much. A quantity of 4,300 treated replacement western red cedar shingles at a cost of £50 were ordered.

Given the uncertainties and difficulties of moving an existing structure, the final invoice for the relocation included '£114 17 2 of extras which were not included for in the original price' with contractor John Grant of Island Farm, Loch Eck, being paid the additional sum of £102 for 'laying stone floor in Hut at Benmore gardens'.

A New Location

The modified Sir Isaac Bayley Balfour Memorial Rest House was re-assembled on the western boundary of the Walled Garden at Benmore. Kelly completed the agreed task with a high degree of skill, craft and dedication. Nonetheless, the understandable decision not to rebuild the hearth and fireplace, together with the external chimney stack, robbed some of the eccentricity from Lorimer's original design. The new location, albeit obviously lacking the drama of Puck's Glen, commands excellent views eastwards across the main vista of the Walled Garden to the hills beyond [fig.26].

Conclusion

RBGE continues to function on a global basis with core objectives to operate as a centre of scientific and horticultural excellence, keeper of the national collections and a promoter of science within the public domain. Collectively, the National Botanic Gardens of Scotland are amongst the most popular of the country's visitor attractions. The present-day garden at Benmore is the largest RBGE site, extending to 49 hectares. There are approximately 13,000 living plants represented by 5,093 accessions. Slightly over half the collection is categorised as wild-collected with specific collection data available, signifying an important asset to support plant conservation strategies and assist scientific research.

Rhododendron, the cornerstone genus of Sir Isaac Bayley Balfour's proposed west coast garden, presently number at Benmore more than 250 species together with a further 100 subspecies. These plants form the backbone of RBGE's *Rhododendron* holdings which comprise the world's richest assemblage of *Rhododendron* species.

Conifers have a long association with Benmore and provide a constant backdrop throughout the garden and wider landscape setting. RBGE grows specimens of 69 per cent of the world's conifer species. Benmore plays a key role in merging science with horticulture to safeguard the genetic diversity of this important group. This ongoing initiative has been co-ordinated from Edinburgh since 1991 by the International Conifer Conservation Programme.

Visitors to Benmore are rewarded with a horticultural experience that reflects every aspect of a rich and varied history. Crossing the bridge over the River Eachaig highlights the unsurpassed avenue of giant redwoods with the nearby ornamental pond and flanking collections of ornamental trees and shrubs awaiting discovery. A vast network of footpaths with adjacent planting ascend the lower slopes of A'Cruach leading to the viewpoint at 137m above sea level, from where the natural order of the post-glacial landscape, including a panoramic view to Puck's Glen, is revealed. More recent collections based around the flora of Tasmania, Bhutan, Chile and Japan retain interest before reaching the recently restored Victorian Fernery building and the remnants of James Duncan's magnificent arboretum in Glen Massan. The entire garden is harmonised by native woodland flowers, mosses, lichens, fungi and ferns.

Sir Isaac Bayley Balfour's position as an insightful and distinguished Regius Keeper of RBGE is secure. His considerable personality and influence intertwine the origins of RBGE at Benmore and the establishment of the Forestry Commission. It is entirely fitting that the major memorial dedicated to his lifetime achievements resides within the woodland and forest landscape of Argyll. Sir Robert Lorimer is remembered for his intuitive design skill and assured handling of varied projects including rustic harled cottages, grander country houses and gardens, the Thistle Chapel and the Scottish National War Memorial. His promotion of the use of homegrown timber and encouragement of the decorative arts in general is worthy of greater recognition.

Fig.27 | *Sir Isaac Bayley Balfour Memorial Rest House (interior) in the Walled Garden at RBGE Benmore, 2020. Photograph by Neil McCheyne.*

Modification of the Sir Isaac Bayley Balfour Memorial Rest House in the late 1960s did not dilute the inherent charm of Lorimer's design. Visitors are instinctively drawn to this much-loved feature of Benmore. It is testament to Lorimer and his craftsmen that a timber building has withstood 90 years of the Argyllshire climate [figs 27 and 28].

A final thought on Lorimer: 'He loved his country, his work, and the things with which it brought him into contact – rough stone and sweet-smelling wood. In these romantic buildings he could give free expression to his impulses'. Puck's Hut, conceived and delivered as a personal tribute, is representative in many ways of the much wider campaign and active debate over many generations to encourage tree planting and reforestation within Scotland. It is a modest structure of national significance. The garden at Benmore remains an integral part of Sir Isaac Bayley Balfour's cherished plan.

Fig.28 | *Sir Isaac Bayley Balfour Memorial Rest House in the Walled Garden at* RBGE *Benmore, 2009. Photograph by Lynsey Wilson.*

Postscript

Sir Robert Lorimer died in September 1929. The Sir Isaac Bayley Balfour Memorial Rest House was amongst the final buildings completed within his lifetime.

Harry George Younger and Sir John Stirling Maxwell are listed amongst the sponsors of George Forrest's final expedition of 1930–2. Shortly after completing his work Forrest suffered a fatal heart attack. He was laid to rest in Tengchong. His plantsmanship and endeavour continue to inspire botanists and horticulturists of each subsequent generation.

Phyllis Bone contributed sculpture and drawings to many exhibitions. She was elected an associate of the Royal Scottish Academy in 1939. Five years later she had the distinction of becoming its first female member.

Sir John Stirling Maxwell continued to support and serve many public bodies and organisations throughout the remainder of his life. In 1931 he concluded a conservation agreement securing the Nether Pollok estate forever for the benefit of the citizens of Glasgow. He died in 1956.

The diligent John D. Sutherland was promoted to the position of Forestry Commissioner in 1935. His attention to detail and fondness for sending letters and memoranda provide vital links to the narrative of Puck's Hut. The visitor book in Benmore House records his frequent visits and affection for the area. In 1950 a stand of Douglas fir at Barcaldine in Argyll was given the name of Sutherland's Grove in his honour.

Sculptor Charles d'Orville Pilkington Jackson enjoyed a long career. He is best remembered for creating the iconic mounted statue of Robert the Bruce (1964) at Bannockburn.

In 1965 the City of Edinburgh Education Authority acquired Benmore House as an Adventure and Expedition Centre. This role continues to the present day with residential courses and accommodation for up to 127 guests.

Scott Morton & Co. Ltd continued to trade until 1966.

The Edinburgh memorial was dismantled when the current front range glasshouse was erected. The inscribed panel is currently built into the wall at the RBGE science buildings, opposite the library. There is a surviving but unused Lorimer drawing (LOR B/29/1/1) associated with the Edinburgh memorial, which is held within Historic Environment Scotland archives.

Sir William Wright Smith's tenure as RBGE Regius Keeper lasted 34 years (1922–56), mirroring exactly the length of service achieved by his predecessor and mentor Sir Isaac Bayley Balfour. The determination of Wright Smith to realise the west coast ambition of RBGE at Benmore was commemorated in 1990 with the construction of a new memorial shelter at the viewpoint designed by Robin Lorimer – grandson of Sir Robert Lorimer.

In 1991 RBGE Regius Keeper Dr David Ingram (b.1941) realised the unfulfilled aim of Sir Isaac Bayley Balfour by signing a memorandum of understanding permitting the development of a 400 sq. m. alpine garden within the remote East Highlands of Scotland.

The significant connection to Sir Robert Lorimer and recognition of the structure as a unique garden building resulted in category c-listing being awarded to the Sir Isaac Bayley Balfour Memorial Rest House by Historic Environment Scotland in June 1992.

The Younger (Benmore) Trust continues to contribute by financing specific projects within the Benmore garden. The Trustees convene twice a year with the incumbent RBGE Regius Keeper as an ex-officio trustee.

By the 1950s the Forestry Commission had become the largest landowner in Scotland and its policies transformed and reshaped the physical appearance of much of the modern countryside. The implementation of plantation-style forestry practices has not gone unchallenged and is not without critics or controversy. The National Forest Estate is currently regulated by Scottish Forestry (an executive agency of the Scottish Government) and promoted as a complex mix of forests and woodlands integrated with wider land-use objectives. In the last 100 years, forest and woodland cover in Scotland has increased to 18.5 per cent. Forestry activities are currently reported to contribute £1 billion per year to the Scottish economy.

The sites at Glenbranter and Puck's Glen are managed by Forestry and Land Scotland. Some of the early *Rhododendron* planting survives at Glenbranter. Kilmun Forest Garden, or Arboretum, continues to be developed and monitored under the guidance of the Research Division. All three sites are open to and can be accessed by the public.

In 2017 the family of William S. Kelly were granted permission to add a commemorative brass plate to Puck's Hut, recording the pride he took in completing the 1968 relocation.

Plans are presently underway to significantly redesign the Walled Garden at Benmore. This work is intended to rejuvenate the area and enhance visitor experience while expanding or diversifying the living collection. Puck's Hut will remain at the heart of the redevelopment.

The octagonal stone dais still marks the original location of Puck's Hut overlooking the gorge at Puck's Glen.

Selected References and Suggested Further Reading

Introduction · page 9

Correspondence between William Wright Smith and Lady Agnes Balfour. Typewritten letter dated 21 January 1925. RBGE Library Archive.

THE GARDENERS' CHRONICLE (1926). Memorial to Sir Isaac Bayley Balfour, 18 December.

Sir Isaac Bayley Balfour · pages 11–14

ANDERSON, MARK L. (1967). *A History of Scottish Forestry*, 2 vols. Thomas Nelson & Sons Ltd, London.

AYRES, P.G. (2015). Isaac Bayley Balfour, Sphagnum Moss and the Great War (1914–18). *Archives of Natural History*, 42(1).

BALFOUR, SIR ISAAC BAYLEY (1894). *Address (on Forestry) to the Biological Section of the British Association*. London.

BOWN, D. (1992). *4 Gardens in One*. HMSO, Edinburgh.

FLETCHER, H.R. & BROWN, W.H. (1970). *The Royal Botanic Garden Edinburgh 1670–1970*. HMSO, Edinburgh.

FOWLER, JOHN (2002). *Landscapes and Lives – The Scottish Forest Through the Ages*. Canongate, Edinburgh.

OOSTHOEK, K. JAN (2013). *Conquering the Highlands*. Australian National University Press, Canberra.

MCLEAN, BRENDA (2004). *George Forrest, Plant Hunter*. Antique Collectors Club, Woodbridge.

PRAIN, SIR DAVID (1924). Obituary Notice of Fellows Deceased, *Transactions and Proceedings of the Royal Society of London*, XCVI-B.

SMOUT, T.C. (1997). Highland Land-Use Before 1800: Misconceptions, Evidence and Realities. In: Smout, T.C. (ed.), *Scottish Woodland History*. Scottish Cultural Press, Edinburgh.

SMOUT, T.C. (ED.) (2003). *People and Woods in Scotland: A History*. Edinburgh University Press, Edinburgh.

The Search for a Suitable Site · pages 15–20

BALFOUR, F.R.S. (1925). Benmore, Argyll, *The Rhododendron Society Notes*, 3(1).

BAYLEY BALFOUR MEMORIAL COMMITTEE (1924). Minute of Meeting, 14 November. RBGE Library Archive, Folder SD55/32, Benmore Puck's Glen, Sir Isaac Bayley Balfour Memorial Correspondence 1923–9.

COWAN, DR JOHN MACQUEEN (c.1933). *Benmore Guidebook*. n.p.

THE GARDENERS' CHRONICLE (1875). Report on Scottish Arboricultural Society, 13 November.

THE GARDENERS' CHRONICLE (1923). Memorial to Sir Isaac Bayley Balfour, 8 December.

J. WATSON LYALL & CO., LAND AGENTS & BLAIR AND FINLAY, W. S. (1889). *Book of Particulars, Plan, and Photograph of the*

Magnificent Highland Domain of Benmore, Bernice, & Kilmun, in Argyllshire. University of Aberdeen Library Archive.

M.V.E. & A.M. (1952). Forestry Commission: History of Benmore Forest 1925–1951. Unpublished report. Available online: https://www.forestry-memories.org.uk/picture/number4143 (accessed September 2019).

NOTES AND QUERIES (1923). Proposed Memorial to Sir Isaac Bayley Balfour. *Transactions of the Royal Scottish Arboricultural Society,* 37.

STALKER, DONALD (1883). Plantations of the Estates of Benmore and Kilmun. *Transactions of the Highland and Agricultural Society of Scotland.* The Royal Highland and Agricultural Society of Scotland, Edinburgh.

Statement of Account, 5 November 1925. RBGE Library Archive, Folder SD55/32, Benmore Puck's Glen, Sir Isaac Bayley Balfour Memorial Correspondence 1923–9.

STIRLING MAXWELL, JOHN (1922). Glenbranter. *The Rhododendron Society Notes,* 2(3).

TRANSACTIONS OF THE ROYAL SCOTTISH ARBORICULTURAL SOCIETY (1914). Report on Tour of Inspection of Woods and Afforestable Lands in Scotland.

WEBSTER, JOHN (1925). Benmore and Kilmun Estates. *Transactions of the Royal Scottish Arboricultural Society,* 39.

WRIGHT SMITH, WILLIAM (1925). Correspondence between William Wright Smith and Mr George Forrest. Typewritten letters dated 24 February 1925 and 31 March 1925. RBGE Library Archive.

WRIGHT SMITH, WILLIAM (1925). Correspondence between William Wright Smith and Sir Lionel Earle (Permanent Secretary to the Office of Works 1912–33). Typewritten letter dated 9 March. RBGE Library Archive.

YOUNGER, DAVID (2004). *Country House Life in the Highlands, The Younger Family at Benmore, 1889–1929.* RBGE, Edinburgh.

Puck's Glen · pages 21–23

J. WATSON LYALL & CO., LAND AGENTS & BLAIR AND FINLAY, W. S. (1889). *Book of Particulars, Plan, and Photograph of the Magnificent Highland Domain of Benmore, Bernice, & Kilmun, in Argyllshire.* University of Aberdeen Library Archive.

MINUTE OF MEETING (1881). *Greenock Natural History Society Book 1874–1881.* Entry for 22 May 1880. Inverclyde Council Archives Ref: GB599/CS2/1/1.

MUNRO, NEIL (1928). *The Bayley Balfour Memorial, Puck's Glen, Benmore, Argyll.* n.p.

STALKER, DONALD (1883). *Plantations of the Estates of Benmore and Kilmun. Transactions of the Highland and Agricultural Society of Scotland.*

SUTHERLAND, JOHN D. (1925). Correspondence between John Sutherland and William Wright Smith. Typewritten letter dated 6 October 1925 and attached Heads of Agreement memorandum. RBGE Library Archive, Folder SD55/32, Benmore Puck's Glen, Sir Isaac Bayley Balfour Memorial Correspondence 1923–9.

The Architect, Contractor and Sculptor · pages 24–33

ANDERSON, CHRISTINA M. (2005). Robert Lorimer & Scott Morton Company, *Regional Furniture*, XIX.

BONE, PHYLLIS (1927). Correspondence between Phyllis Bone and Scott Morton. Handwritten invoice dated 11 November 1927. Edinburgh University Library, Research Collections, Gen 1963/18/199.

CARRUTHERS, ANNETTE (2013). *The Arts and Crafts Movement in Scotland: A History*. Yale University Press, New Haven, CT.

HUSSEY, CHRISTOPHER (1931). *The Work of Sir Robert Lorimer*. Country Life, London.

JACKSON, CHARLES D'ORVILLE PILKINGTON (1928). Correspondence between Charles d'Orville Pilkington Jackson and Sir Robert Lorimer. Typewritten letter dated 16 March 1928. Edinburgh University Library, Research Collections, Gen 1963/18/196.

LORIMER, SIR ROBERT (1899). On Scottish Gardens, *Architectural Review*, November.

LORIMER, SIR ROBERT (1927). Memo regarding Benmore. Typewritten memo dated 12 October 1927. Edinburgh University Library, Research Collections, Gen 1963/18/194.

LORIMER, SIR ROBERT (1928). Correspondence between Sir Robert Lorimer and Charles d'Orville Pilkington Jackson. Typewritten letter dated 27 February 1928. National Library of Scotland, Pilkington Jackson Archive 8542/19/29.

SAVAGE, PETER (1979). The Scottish Gardens of Sir Robert Lorimer, *The Garden – Journal of the Royal Horticultural Society*, 104(8).

SAVAGE, PETER (1980). *Lorimer and the Edinburgh Craft Designers*. Savage Publishers Ltd, London.

SCOTT MORTON & TYNECASTLE CO. LTD (n.d.). Job Book. Historic Environment Scotland, SMO 3/20/20/1.

SCOTT MORTON & TYNECASTLE CO. LTD (1927). Correspondence between Scott Morton & Co. Ltd and Messrs Lorimer & Matthew. Typewritten invoice dated 18 May 1927. Edinburgh University Library, Research Collections, Gen 1963/18/202.

SCOTT MORTON & TYNECASTLE CO. LTD (1927). Correspondence between Scott Morton & Co. Ltd and Messrs Lorimer & Matthew. Typewritten invoice dated 26 December 1927. Edinburgh University Library, Research Collections, Gen 1963/18/198.

SCOTT MORTON & TYNECASTLE CO. LTD (1928). Correspondence between Scott Morton & Co. Ltd and Messrs Lorimer & Matthew. Typewritten estimate dated

7 March 1928. Edinburgh University Library, Research Collections, Gen 1963/18/197.

SUTHERLAND, JOHN D. (1926–7). Correspondence between John Sutherland and Sir Robert Lorimer. Typewritten letters 1926–7. Edinburgh University Library, Research Collections, Gen 1963/18/192, 1963/18/195 & 1963/18/200.

WRIGHT SMITH, WILLIAM (1927). Correspondence between William Wright Smith and Sir John Stirling Maxwell. Typewritten letter dated 11 November 1927. RBGE Library Archive, Folder SD55/32, Benmore Puck's Glen, Sir Isaac Bayley Balfour Memorial Correspondence 1923–9.

Opening · pages 35–8

BUCHAN, JOHN (1931). *Poetry of Neil Munro*. Blackwood and Sons Ltd, Edinburgh.

FLETCHER, H.R. & BROWN, W.H. (1970). *The Royal Botanic Garden Edinburgh 1670–1970*. HMSO, Edinburgh.

KEMP, MARTIN (ED.) (1994). *Mood of the Moment – Masterworks of Photography from the University of St Andrews Exhibition Catalogue*. Crawford Arts Centre, St Andrews.

MCLEAN, BRENDA (2004). *George Forrest, Plant Hunter*. Antique Collectors Club, Woodbridge.

MUNRO, NEIL (1928). *The Bayley Balfour Memorial, Puck's Glen, Benmore, Argyll*. n.p.

PATERSON, LEONIE (2017). RBGE's visionary photographer: Robert Moyes Adam (1885–1967). Available online: https://stories.rbge.org.uk/archives/26906 (accessed October 2018).

Printed invitation to opening of Memorial to Sir Isaac Bayley Balfour, 28 August 1928. RBGE Library Archive, Folder SD55/32, Benmore Puck's Glen, Sir Isaac Bayley Balfour Memorial Correspondence 1923–9.

WRIGHT SMITH, WILLIAM (1928). Correspondence between William Wright Smith and (presumably) the Office of Works. Typewritten Memorandum on Benmore (Balfour Memorial Garden), dated 3 August 1928. RBGE Library Archive.

WRIGHT SMITH, WILLIAM (n.d.). Undated typewritten notes outlining Rules and Regulations in Respect of the Free Admission of the Public to the Bayley Balfour Memorial Arboretum in Puck's Glen. RBGE Library Archive, Folder SD55/32, Benmore Puck's Glen, Sir Isaac Bayley Balfour Memorial Correspondence 1923–9.

The First Forty Years and the Moving of Puck's Hut · pages 38–43

CASSELS, K.A.H. (1967–9). Miscellaneous Correspondence of K. A. H. Cassels (Estate Factor). Typewritten letters 1967–9. Younger (Benmore) Trust Archive, Curator's Office, Benmore.

KELLY, W.S. (1967). Correspondence between W. S. Kelly (Jackson & Kay) and K. A. H. Cassels. Typewritten letter dated 31 August 1967. Younger (Benmore) Trust Archive, Curator's Office, Benmore.

WALTON, JOHN (ED.) (1938). *Guide to the Argyll National Forest Park.* HMSO, London.

WALTON, JOHN (ED.) (1967). *Guide to the Argyll National Forest Park*, 4th edn. HMSO, London.

Conclusion · pages 45–6

Botanic Garden Conservation International (n.d.). Garden search: Royal Botanic Garden Edinburgh. Available online: www.bgci.org/garden.php?id=78 (accessed September 2018).

GIBBS, D., CHAMBERLAIN, D. & ARGENT, G. (2011). *The Red List of Rhododendrons*, Botanic Gardens Conservation International, Richmond.

HUSSEY, CHRISTOPHER (1931). *The Works of Sir Robert Lorimer,* Country Life, London.

Postscript · pages 48–9

CUMMING, ELIZABETH (2018). *Phyllis M Bone – Animal Sculptor.* Georgian Antiques, Edinburgh.

DEVINE, T.M. (1999). *The Scottish Nation 1700–2000.* Penguin Books Ltd, London.

FERGUSON, ROBERT (2017). *Pollok House,* National Trust for Scotland, Edinburgh.

GIFFORD, JOHN & WALKER, FRANK ARNEIL (2002). *Buildings of Scotland, Stirling & Central,* Yale University Press, New Haven, CT.

MASON, W.L., CAIRNS, P. & TRACY, D.R. (1999). Kilmun Forest Garden – A Review. *Scottish Forestry,* 53(4).

RACKHAM, OLIVER (2015). *Woodlands.* William Collins, London.

SCOTLAND'S FORESTRY STRATEGY (2019–29). Available online: https://www.gov.scot/publications/scotlands-forestry-strategy-20192029 (accessed March 2020).

Appendix

An undated four-page fundraising brochure entitled
'Proposed Memorial to Sir Isaac Bayley Balfour' was donated
to RBGE Library Archives by Mr Edward Aglen on 24 April
1990. Listed within the brochure are the 32 influential
members of a large General Committee. Private donations
from some individuals within the group have been identified,
but the records are incomplete.

General Committee

Mr F.R.S. Balfour

Dr A.W. Borthwick

Professor F.O. Bower

Mr R. Cory

Professor W.G. Craib

The Earl of Crawford and Balcarres

Mr Lionel de Rothschild MP

Sir Lionel Earle

Mr Charles Eley

Viscount Esher

Sir Alfred Ewing

Professor J.B. Farmer

Mr George Forrest

Colonel W.S. Fotheringham

Mr A. Grove

Dr A.W. Hill

Colonel H.H. Johnston

Sir Frederick W. Keeble

M. Lecomte

Mr Gerald Loder

Sir Herbert Maxwell

Hon. H.D. McLaren MP

Sir Frederick Moore

The Earl of Moray

Sir David Prain

Dr A.B. Rendle

Professor A.C. Seward

Mr A.A. Dorrien Smith

Professor W.W. Smith

Sir John Stirling Maxwell

Mr John Sutherland

Mr J.C. Williams

Acknowledgements

I am extremely grateful to the members of the Younger (Benmore) Trust who kindly read and commented on my early draft text, in particular Mike Thornley who generously provided guidance and encouragement throughout the editing process. Publication of this book has been made possible by support from the Trust.

A special thank you to Kate Hughes (RBGE Horticultural Project Officer) who offered positive feedback at a critical stage and identified the skilled production team necessary to make this book a reality.

I would like to thank RBGE Library staff members Lorna Mitchell (Head of Library Services) and Leonie Paterson (Archivist) for their help and support in researching this book. I am indebted to Graham Hardy (Serials Librarian) who quietly coped with my numerous requests and kindly arranged image reproduction consents upon my behalf. Simon Spanton (RBGE Publications) provided much appreciated advice and support.

The draft form of this book would not have been completed without expert help from the staff of many other institutions: Dawn Evers (Library Manager) and Joe Waterfield (Public Services Officer), both from Historic Environment Scotland; Paul Fleming, Danielle Spittle and Stephen Willis (Library Assistants) from the Edinburgh University Library Centre for Research Collections (CRC); Robin Rodger (Documentation Officer) from the Royal Scottish Academy of Art and Architecture; Jamie McIntosh (Special Collections Library Assistant) from the National Library of Scotland; James McDougall (Promotion and Events Manager) from Forestry Scotland;

Gordon Donaldson (Cowal and Trossachs Forest District Manager) from Forest and Land Scotland; Lorraine Murray (Archivist) from Inverclyde Council; Jane Campbell (Research Cataloguer and Database Officer) from University of St Andrews Library Special Collections; and staff at University of Aberdeen Library Archive.

Thank you to photographer Lynsey Wilson (RBGE) who kindly restored, formatted and supplied images to help illustrate this work. Norman Davidson offered much appreciated advice regarding sourcing and crediting images.

I am extremely grateful to Dr Andrew Watson for his kind generosity in sharing his research into James Piers Patrick and James Duncan at Benmore, and in particular for drawing my attention to the entry within the Minute Book of the Greenock Natural History Society.

Special thanks to interpretive design consultant Shirley Lochhead of Tea and Type for kind permission to reproduce her original artwork.

Locally I am indebted to Peter Baxter (Garden Curator), Neil McCheyne (Garden Supervisor) and Sybil Gray (Administration Officer), all from RBGE at Benmore; Graeme Adams (Operations Manager) from Benmore Outdoor Centre; Pam Horton (Manager) from Dunoon Public Library and her staff; Gill Wollers (*Dunoon Observer/ argyllmedia.co.uk*); and Vicky Kelly and the family of William S. Kelly.

The production team of Nye Hughes (Dalrymple), Dai Noble (Gomer Press) and Anna Stevenson (copyediting and proofreading) provided friendly support and advice throughout the planning and preparation of this work. Their skill and attention to detail is greatly appreciated.